WHOSE REPORT WILL YOU BELIEVE?

DISCOVER KEYS TO UNLEASHING SUPERNATURAL BREAKTHROUGHS IN YOUR LIFE

THE ROCK PUBLISHING

BRUSSELS, BELGIUM

WHOSE REPORT WILL YOU BELIEVE?

DISCOVER KEYS TO UNLEASHING SUPERNATURAL BREAKTHROUGHS IN YOUR LIFE

BY

RICHARD ONEBAMOI

"For I know the thoughts that I think toward you, saith the LORD, thoughts of peace, and not of evil, to give you an expected end." (Jeremiah 29:11)

I present to you "Whose Report Will You Believe?" It is my prayer that the Holy Spirit will use it to speak timeless truth to your heart in a fresh new way, causing the floodgates of heaven to open unto you.

Whose Report Will You Believe?:
Discover Keys To Unleashing Supernatural Breakthroughs In Your Life

Copyright © 2019 by Richard Onebamoi

ISBN: 978-9-0812-6362-7
D/2008/11,789/2

Richard Onebamoi International
P.O. Box 30
1200 Brussels
Belgium

E-mail: info@richardonebamoi.com
Websites: www.richardonebamoi.com.

Published by The ROCK Publishing
Richard Onebamoi
P.O. Box 30
1200 Brussels
Belgium

Printed in Belgium

All rights reserved under International Copyright Law. Contents and cover may not be reproduced in whole or in part in any form without the express written permission of the Publisher.

To find out more about this book or the author, visit
www.richardonebamoibooks.com

Join My Reader's List

Sign up for notification of new books by Richard Onebamoi and exclusive giveaway.
https://www.richardonebamoibooks.com/

Check Out The Latest Release By Richard Onebamoi

God's Word My Guarantee: Unleashing the Power of God's Word in Your Life

Table of Contents

Dedication --- vii
Preface --- ix

Chapter One
    By Two Immutable Things --- 13

Chapter Two
    The Faithfulness of God --- 23

Chapter Three
    God's Report versus Man's Report --- 31

Chapter Four
    Making the Impossible Possible! --- 41

Chapter Five
    God's Word Brings Change --- 53

Chapter Six
    Hope Comes Through God's Word --- 61

Chapter Seven
    The Place of God's Word --- 69

Chapter Eight
    The Battle is Not Yours, But the Victory --- 79

Chapter Nine
    Not by Might, Not by Power But by My Spirit --- 85

Chapter Ten
    Engaging Divine Clearance For Signs & Wonders --- 95

Kingdom Covenant Partner --- 103
About the Author --- 105
Thank You --- 107

Dedication

I wish to dedicate this book and extend my sincerest thanks to the strong leadership of faithful men and women who have tirelessly served over the years, without which it would have been challenging to accomplish the vision.

May Jehovah God stretches forth His mighty hand upon you and continually grace and empower you to function and fulfill your prophetic assignment and destiny.

PREFACE

This book identifies the errors that bring us to believe the enemy's reports instead of believing God's. Therefore, it is imperative to know that you cannot afford to stand between lines or be ignorant of the enemy's strategies. When you become conscious of whose and what report you believe, with the understanding that it determines and affects your life and those of your loved ones, you will be encouraged to believe and hold tenaciously onto the right report, "the report of the Lord."

The scripture declares in Isaiah 53:1, "Who hath believed our report and to whom is the arm of the Lord revealed?" The New Living Translation puts it thus: "Who has believed our message? To whom will the LORD reveal his saving power?" Whose and what report or message you believe will ultimately determine whose arm (strength and power) that will be revealed or manifested on your behalf. You will find comfort in God's Word, knowing that "With men it is impossible, but not with God: for with God all things are possible." (Mark 10:27)

Consequently, if you believe the report of the Lord — the arm of the Lord, which is the awesome and saving power of God — His authority, His protection, His mercy, and forgiveness will become active and manifested on your behalf. You know it is possible to be born-again and talking in tongues and yet be blind to the promises of God and your covenant rights.

The Apostle Paul in Ephesians 1:18 was motivated to pray for the Church at Ephesus, saying, "The eyes of your understanding being enlightened; that ye may know what is the hope of his calling, and what the riches of the glory of his inheritance in the saints." It is, therefore, my humble prayer that as you read this book, Whose Report Will You Believe?, It will illuminate the eyes of your understanding concerning your covenant rights, privileges, and inheritance in the beloved.

I strongly and prayerfully recommend this book to you and your loved ones, for it will bless you immeasurably.

Richard ONEBAMOI

> GOD IS NOT A MAN, THAT HE SHOULD LIE; NEITHER THE SON OF MAN, THAT HE SHOULD REPENT: HATH HE SAID, AND SHALL HE NOT DO IT? OR HATH HE SPOKEN, AND SHALL HE NOT MAKE IT GOOD?
>
> NUMBERS 23:19

CHAPTER ONE

WHOSE REPORT WILL YOU BELIEVE?

BY TWO IMMUTABLE THINGS

"Wherein God, willing more abundantly to shew unto the heirs of promise the immutability of his counsel, confirmed it by an oath: That by two immutable things, in which it was impossible for God to lie, we might have a strong consolation, who have fled for refuge to lay hold upon the hope set before us." (Hebrews 6: 17-18)

God's promise to Abraham was "surely blessing I will bless thee, and multiplying I will multiply thee, and because He could not swear by no one greater, He swore by Himself." (Hebrews 6: 13-14) The word *"swear"* is the Hebrew word **"Shaba"** (Strong H7650), which implies to swear, to give one's word, to bind oneself by an oath while the Greek word is known as **"hórkos"** (Strong G3727), which means *"to affirm, promise or threaten with an oath, in swearing to call a person or thing as witness."* Therefore, when the writer of Hebrews used this word in the preceding text, he was implying that God completely bound Himself with an oath and is calling Himself as a witness to what He has promised.

The Lord yearns to reveal to you the immutability of His counsel (His unchangeable will and purposes) for your life, and He confirms it by taking an oath on Himself, thus by these two immutable things, it is impossible for God to lie. God's Word over your situation cannot lie, and it will affect that situation and turn it around for your good.

God's Word declares that by two immutable things, it is impossible for the Almighty God to lie or deny Himself of what He has purposed to do or accomplish in your life. Thus, implying that if God said He was going to heal you, deliver you, bless and protect you, that Word is sure, guaranteed and cannot change.

What are these two immutable things? They are:

(1) God's Word (Promise) and

(2) God's Oath.

When God made a promise to Abraham, He did not only speak but also took an oath to confirm the promise He made to Abraham. This serves as the guarantee and seal of what He said. On the human level, to keep a promise, we swear on a higher authority. Even though in many cases, human commitments are rarely adhered to, we swear by someone greater, which is a confirmation to us and an end to strife.

God, on the other hand, could not swear by any greater or lesser, for heaven is His habitation, and the earth is His footstool. My God! There was none beside Him; neither was there any above Him. The Almighty God took an oath upon Himself and declared that "I am" and "I will." This ensures that his report concerning you shall come to fruition.

Isaiah 45:23 *states "I have sworn by myself, the word is gone out of my mouth in righteousness, and shall not return, That unto me every knee shall bow, every tongue shall swear."* Child of God, since God does not and cannot lie, and He is all-powerful, He will fulfill His Word. The unchanging nature of God and His Word is the believer's comfort and confidence that these two immutable things secure your destiny secured in God. In Jeremiah 29: 11, we read God's report: *"For I know the thoughts that I think toward you, saith the Lord, thoughts of peace, and not of evil, to give you an expected end."*

It is our ignorance of God's Word, which He reports concerning your healing, prosperity, holiness, deliverance, and your inheritance in the beloved that robbed you for this long. Allow me to challenge you to get into God's Word for yourself. Discover and take hold of the precious promises of God, appropriating them in your life, confessing them and claiming them by faith today. They are yours and yours to be possessed.

TRUTH VERSUS FACTS

"Then said Jesus to those Jews which believed on him, if you continue in my word, then are you, my disciples, indeed; And ye shall know the truth, and the truth shall make you free." (John 8: 31-32)

Do you live according to truth or facts? Are you governed by your circumstances or standing on God's Word and His promise? The truth is not susceptible to change, but the facts are. Truth is based on God's Word, His promise, and not on circumstantial evidence. The fact is based on circumstantial evidence and not on God's Word. For example, it is a fact that you are poor or sick, but the truth is *"For ye know the grace of our Lord Jesus Christ, that, though he was rich, yet for your sakes he became poor, that through his poverty might be rich" (2 Corinthians 8:9).* In other words, He became poor, that you might be rich and *"Who his own self bare our sins in his own body on the tree, that we, being dead to sins, should live unto righteousness: by whose stripes ye were healed."* (1 Peter 2:24), that is, you are healed by the stripes that were laid upon Jesus Christ. It is vital to understand what God's Word says about you and all your concerns.

God's Word about you is the eternal truth and what the doctors or circumstances declare are just facts that are detailed and subject to change at any given point in time. The scripture offers us understanding in Jeremiah 29:11, *"The thoughts of God towards us are of peace, and not of evil, with an unequivocal purpose to bring us to an expected end."* That is His plans and intentions for your life, and it will ultimately come to fruition and prevail over the works of the enemy. Consequently, sickness, diseases, and poverty are not your portion and not in the will of God concerning you and your loved ones.

In this world, things are unstable and unpredictable. Uncertainty looms on every side, even though human technological soars, all these human developments are unable to respond to the issues that plague humanity. It is as apparent today as it was in the past. We need a higher source of power to depend on at all times. That source of power is the unchanging and the uncompromising Word of God and the oath He took upon Himself, **"by these two**

immutable things." Rest assured, my friends; God will never leave you nor forsake you, for He will come through for you in Jesus' Name.

DIRECTION THROUGH CONFIDENCE IN GOD'S WORD

> *"Behold, the LORD thy God hath set the land before thee: go up and possess it, as the LORD God of thy fathers hath said unto thee; fear not, neither be discouraged. And ye came near unto me every one of you, and said, we will send before us, and they shall search us out the land, and bring us word by what way we must go up, and into what cities we shall come." (Deuteronomy 1:21-22)*

We notice in the above scriptural text that the children of Israel, who were resolved in their minds, requested spies to be sent out to search out the land, which the Lord had previously promised to them for their possession. The dialogue, as well as the activities, undertaken by the children of Israel, was an indication that they lacked the knowledge and the understanding of the counsel of God, which ultimately was unbelief in God's Word. This, of course, led to planning and acting on their initiative.

Child of God, whenever you do not understand the counsel and the mind of God, whatever you do then becomes an <u>alternative</u> to what God had already promised you. Unbelief, therefore, is not acknowledging and acting on God's Word. Furthermore, disbelief is going your way, choosing what you see as popular and preferred by the majority at the expense of God's Word.

Moses went to God with the request of the children of Israel (or better said, their <u>demands</u>) possibly not knowing the profundity of unbelief embedded in their hearts. However, God, who weighs the thoughts and intents of man's heart, gave them up to their reprobate mind, to do those things which they appraised convenient and pleasing to them.

This same situation is true today in the lives of many sincere children of God. We often do not take God at His word or believe His promises for us. Most of the time, we often choose to believe man's report and what the circumstances dictate. This is a reflection of our unbelief and rebelliousness against God and His Word. It is imperative to understand that absolute confidence in God's Word is a prerequisite to experiencing the promises of God. Upon close examination of the situation, we find conclusive evidence that unbelief was embedded in their hearts.

Search out the land: God's covenant was to bring the children of Israel to the land of promise. God had already searched out the land, which flows with milk and honey, but they chose to believe the report of the spies, and walk by sight rather than by faith in the report of the Lord.

Bring us a word: From the scriptural passages above, we discover that God had previously spoken His Word to them, but the children of Israel still desired a word from man, irrespective of God's Word. This indicates that they had more confidence in the words of men than in the Word of God.

The way we must go: God had already made the provision. They seeking out a new course of action for themselves is a demonstration of their lack of confidence in His directions and guidance. Despite the miracles they experienced when God delivered them from the land of bondage, (such as the pillar of cloud and fire, the manna from heaven, the parting of the Red Sea and the sweetening of the bitter water at Mara), they still chose not to accept God's direction.

To what cities shall we come: God had already chosen the city. However, to them, the city selected by the spies was most appropriate. This corroborates the fact that they had no confidence in God's judgment.

The scriptures declare in the book of Numbers 13:1-2, *"And the Lord spake unto Moses, saying, send thou men, that they may search the land of Canaan, which I give unto the children of Israel: of every tribe of their fathers shall ye send a man, everyone a ruler among them."* Here, we see Moses sending out men to explore the land of Canaan at the command of God. God promised the children of Israel that He was going to bring them into a land flowing with milk and honey. One would think that God meant what He said and said what He meant, without the help of spies.

Notwithstanding, the children of Israel did not see it in this context, but requested and inclined themselves to sending spies into the land before stepping out in faith to occupy the land. Understand that it was not God's initiative neither was it Moses' to send spies into the land, but the initiative of the people of Israel.

It is imperative to know that different people react in different ways when they are subjected to the same situations or circumstances. However, these reactions should be based on the amount of knowledge of God's Word that is possessed. For instance, the other ten men that brought the evil report with Joshua and Caleb were given the same instructions and subjected to the same situation. They all saw the same things, the same people, and spied on the same land, but the perceptions and reactions of the ten men were quite different from those of Joshua and Caleb.

On the other hand, the multitude that remained at home believed the evil report because their mindset was that the majority is right, even if what the majority believes runs counter to God's Word. This is also apparently seen today in our individual and collective lives as children of God. What we see around us today is similar to what we read about the children of Israel in those days.

WHAT COULD BE RESPONSIBLE FOR THIS GLARING DIFFERENCE BETWEEN THESE MEN?

- All twelve spies heard God's report, but Joshua and Caleb <u>believed</u> God's report.
- Ten of the spies saw themselves in the perspective of the prevailing circumstances.
- Joshua and Caleb saw themselves from the perspective of God's report (His Word).
- Joshua and Caleb kept God's report (His Word) in their hearts.
- Joshua and Caleb meditated on God's report (God's Word).
- The ten spies acted out of fear, while Joshua and Caleb acted out of faith upon God's Word.
- Joshua and Caleb had another spirit
- Joshua and Caleb spoke out of the conviction they had based on the report of the Lord.

Our Lesson

God's Word was Joshua and Caleb's standard of measure in every circumstance.

BEHOLD, HE THAT KEEPETH ISRAEL SHALL NEITHER SLUMBER NOR SLEEP

PSALMS 121:4

CHAPTER TWO

WHOSE REPORT WILL YOU BELIEVE?

THE FAITHFULNESS OF GOD

"Let us hold fast the profession of our faith without wavering; (for he is faithful that promised)." (Hebrews 10:23)

The above scriptural text lets us understand that God is a promise-keeper. God's faithfulness is one of His most essential attributes, and that faithfulness is widespread throughout scripture. He stays true to His Word and is inseparable from His faithfulness. In God's faithfulness, we have the surety and confidence that He will perform that which His love has led Him to promise to those who obey the Word.

On this premise, you can believe and hold on unwaveringly to the report of the Lord. Our Heavenly Father will also fulfill what His holiness (justice) has led Him to promise to the disobedient. In other words, God is faithful to His word despite the situation or condition. God's faithfulness precedes all that he says and does. Hence, he will not deny himself what he has declared because of man's failure.

God's faithfulness is seen in **keeping His promise**: In 1 Kings 8:56 we read, *"Blessed be the LORD, that hath given rest unto his people Israel, according to all that he promised: there hath not failed one word of all his good promise, which he promised by the hand of Moses, his servant."* Indeed, not one word of His promise was left unfulfilled, and God's promise to you will not be left unfulfilled.

God proves faithful in keeping His promise, and His faithfulness endures forever. He does what He says and says what He does. The Apostle Peter further elucidates, *"The Lord is not slack concerning his promise, as some men count slackness; but is longsuffering toward us, not willing that any should perish, but that all should come to repentance."* (2 Peter 3:9) The reason you should be able to hold fast to the confession of your faith without wavering or being double-minded is the eternal truth **that He that has promised is FAITHFUL.**

Besides the challenges you might be faced with or the arsenals, the enemy has arrayed against you, no matter what the circumstance that confronts you right now, rest assured that God's promises for your life must come to fruition for HE is faithful and all things work together for the good of those that love Him. Despite your unfaithfulness, **God remains faithful.**

Child of God, understand that Jehovah demonstrates His faithfulness in keeping His promises. What He has promised to you in His Word, He shall perform if you do not waiver or stagger at His promise. Abraham, our father of faith, did not stagger at God's promise through unbelief. *"He staggered not at the promise of God through unbelief; but was strong in faith, giving glory to God."* (Romans 4:20) Our knowledge of the faithfulness of God empowers us to believe His report and preserves us from worry, doubt, and unbelief. The assurance that God is faithful to His Word puts our complaining and murmurings at a check and increases our confidence in Him and the integrity of His Word.

THERE SHALL BE A PERFORMANCE

"Then said Mary unto the angel, How shall this be, seeing I know not a man? And the angel answered and said unto her, The Holy Ghost shall come upon thee, and the power of the Highest shall overshadow thee: therefore also that holy thing which shall be born of thee shall be called the Son of God." (Luke 1:34-35)

There was a young virgin called Mary in the land of Judah, who was betrothed to a young man by the name of Joseph. One day, this young lady, had a visitation from an angel with a message that she would bear a son who will be the Savior of the world. This kind of news would be anticipated and appreciated by any young lady, but there is just one concern — she knew no man and this condition made the message even more astonishing and disturbing to this young virgin. To her finite mind, as well as her natural inclination, having a child was a natural phenomenon that requires a biological father and mother.

The message of the angel, however, overwhelmed her so incredibly that she queried, *"How shall this be seeing I know no man?"* This question revealed her state of mind and her thought process that indicated that for such to happen of necessity, there must be a man. In her mind, this would be an impossible occurrence. Most believers often respond in such manner when a word of prophecy or a declaration of God's promises upon them; the question that often comes to mind is how shall this be? Also, can this be done and not to mention other series of questions that are the results of being familiar with prevailing circumstances. This ought not to be so.

All the same, the angel responded to her query and said, *"The Holy Ghost shall come upon thee, and the power of the highest shall overshadow thee: therefore also that holy thing which shall be born of thee shall be called the Son of God."* The angel also said to Mary, "Behold your cousin Elizabeth, she has also conceived a son in her old age; and this is the sixth month with her, who was called barren. For with God nothing shall be impossible."

I believe that Mary finally received God's Word and came to the understanding of the omnipotence of God, and this gave her the courage to line up with the Word of God. She made a declaration of her faith by saying, *"Let it be done unto me according to thy word. And the angel departed from her"*. (Luke 1:38b).

There is a word from God for you today. Whose report will you believe? Man's report about your circumstances or God's report and His declared intent for your life?

Friends, no matter what conditions your life is in, as you align with God's intents for your life, have the assurance that nothing shall be impossible unto you. It shall be done unto you and your family, according to His Word, because God is faithful to His Word. I assure you that His Spirit will brood over your life and His power from on high will overshadow you, and there shall be a performance of His Word in your life. Again, I say there shall be <u>a performance in your life in Jesus' name!</u>

In Luke 1:45, we read, *"And blessed is she that believed: for there shall be a performance of those things, which were told her from the Lord."* The word **blessed** implies **to be empowered**. Replacing "blessed" with "empowered" the text would now read, "empowered is he/she that believed" (Author's emphasis). As you believe God's Word and as the Holy Ghost overshadows you, you will become empowered. The Greek word for *performance* is **teleiosis** (Strong G5050), which denotes a *"fulfillment", "completion", "perfection," "the event which verifies a promise"* to carry through completely", "to accomplish", finish", and "bring to an end" "an end accomplished as the effect of a process" or "an event which verifies the promise." With the announcement to Mary that her aged cousin, who had been barren for years, was with child, she straightaway left to see her.

On her arrival, something extraordinary took place. As soon as Elizabeth heard the salutation of Mary, the baby in her womb leaped for joy. Elizabeth, being filled with the Holy Spirit, began to prophecy saying, *"And blessed is she that believed: for there shall be a performance of those things which were told her from the Lord."* (Luke 1:45).

In other words, there shall be a fulfillment and completion of that which the Lord has spoken to Mary. Child of God, you must understand, no matter the condition or situation you face in life, you must take advantage of God's Word and discover what it says about you. God's Word declares in Jeremiah 29:11, *"For I know the thoughts that I think toward you, saith the Lord, thoughts of peace, and not of evil, to give you an expected end."* (This text is worth repeating here.) There shall be a performance of God's Word in your life as you believe, and God's utmost desire is to bring you to an expected end. Be encouraged, my friend, for with God, nothing shall be impossible, and nothing shall be impossible to him that believes, for God's Word is your final arbiter and report.

NOW UNTO HIM THAT IS ABLE TO DO EXCEEDING ABUNDANTLY ABOVE ALL THAT WE ASK OR THINK, ACCORDING TO THE POWER THAT WORKETH IN US,

EPHESIANS 3:20

CHAPTER THREE

WHOSE REPORT WILL YOU BELIEVE?

GOD'S REPORT VERSUS MAN'S REPORT

"Who hath believed our report? and to whom is the arm of the LORD revealed." (Isaiah 53:1)

"Who has believed our message? To whom will the LORD reveal his saving power?" (New Living Translation)

Whose report will you believe? The New Living Translation puts it thus: *"Who has believed our message? To whom will the LORD reveal his saving power?"* Whose message will you believe? God's report or Man's report; God's Word or your circumstance? Whose and what report or message you believe will ultimately determine whose arm (strength and power) will be revealed or manifested on your behalf.

You can find solace in God's Word knowing that: *"With men it is impossible, but not with God: for with God all things are possible* (Mark 10:27)." Hence, if you believe the report of the Lord, the arm of the Lord, which is the miraculous and saving power of God, His authority, His protection, His mercy, and forgiveness, will be activated and manifested on your behalf.

Whatever you are going through or your conditions in life, (whether you are sick, oppressed, tormented or poor), do not believe the reports of the doctors, circumstances or man's opinion and judgment of the situation. Believe and tenaciously hold onto God's report and His evaluation of the situation, for God's report is the final arbiter for whatever you are going through. The report of the Lord says you are healed, delivered, set free, and prosperous. Be bold to align yourself with God's report by declaring with your mouth and believing in your heart what your mouth confesses.

GOD'S REPORT

God's report is His Word, His will, and His purpose. In the events of life, irrespective of the situations or circumstances that occur, what God says is His report, and it will ultimately stand unaltered and efficacious if you believe and take heed and adhere to it. The apostle Paul declared, *"... for I know whom I have believed, and am persuaded that he is able to keep that which I have committed unto him against that day".* (2 Timothy 1:12). Brother Paul was immensely convinced about the report of the Lord that he believed in the fulfillment of what God has promised. You have to be fully persuaded in the report of the Lord to see God's Word come to Fruition in your life.

The scripture declares, *"I know the thoughts that I think toward you, saith the LORD, thoughts of peace, and not of evil, to give you an expected end."* (Jeremiah 29:11). The New Living Translation puts it thus: *"For I know the plans I have for you, says the LORD. They are plans for good and not for disaster, to give you a future and a hope."* This is God's report concerning you, your family, and every aspect of your life despite the challenges that you are encountering. God's report has innate ability to render ineffective all the works of the enemy and all attempts to sabotage your success.

It is imperative to know and be sure of this very fact that God's report is not based on circumstance; neither does it depend on what we go through or do not go through in life. God's report about our circumstances or situations must be held tenaciously to experience the fulfillment of the promises of His Word and the burden-lifting and yoke-destroying power of God.

Man's Report

Man's report is his word, will, and personal agendas. Man's report depends on what he can feel, touch, taste, and see. This is man's evaluation of our world. This so-called sophisticated thought pattern, opinion, and reasoning of man, which are void of the complete counsel of God's Word.

Numbers 13:32 says *"And they brought up an evil report of the land which they had searched unto the children of Israel, saying, The land, through which we have gone to search it, is a land that eateth up the inhabitants thereof; and all the people that we saw in it are men of a great stature."* The Scripture identifies such as evil reports, no matter how reasonable they might seem. Why is man's report referred to as evil? Because the word of God is his will, so if your thought patterns and reasoning are not in line with God's

Word, they do not conform to His will and so are referred to as evil.

Man's report is established on the superfluity of naughtiness, circumstantial evidence that contradicts the absolute counsel and integrity of God's word while God's report is the infallible counsel of his heart and the rock on which we stand, which we can depend on and which can save our souls. Man's report can also be attributed to past experiences and what he has learned from it, which now become his guiding principle that ultimately disregards God's report as he authenticates his experience above God's report.

NOW FAITH IS

> "Now faith is the substance of things hoped for, the evidence of things not seen." (Hebrews 11:1)

> "Now faith is the assurance (the confirmation, the title deed) of the things (we) hope for, being the proofs of things (we) do not see and the conviction of their reality (faith perceiving as real fact what is not revealed to the senses)." (Amplified Bible)

The understanding of the scriptural text above depicts that faith considers things "hoped for" as authentic and as the proof or conviction of what we do not see. Biblical faith is not a persuasion that results from the outcome of imagination, but that, which depend on God's Word.

Let us examine the following words, *substance,* and *evidence* in Hebrews11:1. The Greek word for *substance* is **Hypóstasis** (Strong's G5287), and it is made up of two compound words **Hypó** (Strong's G5259), meaning *"under,"* and **Hístēmi** (Strong's G2476), meaning *"hold up," to stand firm."* Therefore, **Hypóstasis** implies that *"which underlines the apparent, essence or reality, support, groundwork, confidence, confirmation, title deed, that which is the basis of something, that which becomes a foundation for another thing to stand on."*

Additionally, Thayer's Greek Lexicon defines *Hypóstasis* as *"a setting or placing under; thing put under, substructure, foundation: that which has a foundation, is firm; hence, that which has actual existence; a substance, real being."* Faith, therefore, is that which holds up, that which you are hoping for but have not yet seen.

On the other hand, the Greek word for *evidence* is **"élengchos"** (Strong's G1650). It is a legal term meaning *"evidence that is accepted for conviction, proof, that by which a thing is proved or tested, conviction or persuasion of things not seen, demonstration or manifestation."* Therefore, *Élenchos* implies *"that by which we readily perceive or apprehend what we do not see based on God's Word producing something that furnishes proof."*

Furthermore, Thayer's Greek Lexicon defines *elengchos* as that by which invisible things are proved or tested, and we are persuaded of their reality. Just as your physical eyesight is the sense that gives you evidence of the material world, so also faith is the sense that provides you evidence of the invisible, the things you hope for but not yet seen. Our faith is the proof, conviction, or persuasion of what we are hoping for or believing God will do and that we have received what we hope for even when it is not physically visible.

Apostle Paul further emphasizes in 2 Corinthians 4: 18 NKJV that *"While we do not look at the things which are seen, but at the things which are not seen. For the things which are seen are temporary; but the things which are not seen are eternal."* Your human senses deal with things that are temporal and changeable, but faith deals with things that are invisible, eternal, and unchanging, which is unperceivable to man's physical senses.

The phrase *"things hoped for"* comes from the Greek word **"Elpizó"** (Strong's G1679), which means *"to hope, to have a favorable and confident expectation."* Things hoped for always exist beyond the realm of visibility, that which cannot be seen or perceived with the natural senses. However, its non-visibility is not an indication of its non-existence. This suggests that things hoped for, yet not seen or experienced in the physical, exist in the supernatural and have higher tangibility than the things seen or experienced in the material world.

The substance (essence or reality, title deed, support or ground work), the evidence (proof, that by which a thing is proved, tested or convicted) of things hoped for and yet not seen is *faith*. Scriptural faith treats things hoped for as real, the proof or manifestation of what is unseen as being real. In reality, for faith to be activated, it is necessary to hope for things. This suffices to say that a lack of things hoped for could be one of the reasons why many believers are not experiencing the potency of faith and its demonstration in their lives. It is imperative to understand, therefore, that the report of the Lord is the substance of things hoped for, the evidence of things not seen.

What is your situation right now that is militating against you? All you have to do is locate the Word of the Lord, which is His report concerning that situation and stand upon it, believe it and confess it and the arm of the Lord will be revealed to you.

WALK BY FAITH AND NOT BY SIGHT

"For we walk by faith, not by sight." (2 Corinthians 5:7)

"For we walk by faith (we regulate our lives and conduct ourselves by our conviction or belief respecting man's relationship to God and divine things, with trust and holy fervor; thus we walk) not by sight or appearance." (Amplified Bible)

"So shall my word be that goeth out of my mouth: it shall not return to me void, but shall accomplish that which I please, and it shall prosper in the thing whereto I sent it." (Isaiah 55:11)

"It is the same with my word. I send it out, and it always produces fruit. It will accomplish all I want it to, and it will prosper everywhere I send it." (New Living Translation)

The Greek word for *"walk"* is **Peripateō** (Strong's G4043), meaning "to regulate one's life" or "to conduct one's self." The Greek word for *"sight"* is **Eidos** (Strong's G1491), meaning that which strikes the eyes, that which is exposed to view or external appearance. Not walking by sight simply means we are not to conduct the affairs of our lives based on what we see with the eyes in the natural. Instead, we are to conduct ourselves based on the infallible Word of God and that is what it means to walk by faith.

The scripture admonishes us to walk by faith and not by sight. We understand that faith comes because of God's Word. Walking by faith (hearing and receiving), therefore, is walking by the Word of God. It would suffice to say that we ought to conduct and regulate our lives in the light of God's Word. Consequently, walking by sight means to conduct our lives by what strikes the eyes, and what is exposed to our view or external appearances, which are often contrary to God's Word.

In Hebrews 11:6, we read, *"But without faith, it is impossible to please him: for he that cometh to God must believe that he is, and that he is a rewarder of them that diligently seek him."* God has spoken to us explicitly that without faith, it is impossible to please Him. To believe the report of the Lord, you have to have faith in God. The man or woman that comes to God must believe that He is a rewarder of those who seek Him diligently.

It takes much more than the confession of faith to walk by faith genuinely. We must be resolved ardently in our hearts with the conviction that what goes out of the mouth of God will not return to Him void and His Word will accomplish that which God pleases and prospers in the purpose for which it was sent. (See Isaiah 55:10-11).

> AS THE MOUNTAINS ARE ROUNDABOUT JERUSALEM, THE LORD IS ROUNDABOUT HIS PEOPLE FROM HENCEFORTH EVEN FOREVER.
>
> PSALM 125:2

Chapter Four

Whose Report Will You Believe?

Making the Impossible Possible!

"And a certain woman, which had an issue of blood twelve years, and had suffered many things of many physicians, and had spent all that she had, and was nothing bettered, but rather grew worse, When she had heard of Jesus, came in the press behind, and touched his garment. For she said, 'If I may touch but his clothes, I shall be whole'. And straightway the fountain of her blood was dried up; and she felt in her body that she was healed of that plague". (Mark 5:25-29)

"And, behold, a woman, which was diseased with an issue of blood twelve years, came behind him, and touched the hem of his garment." (Matthew 9:20)

The situation of the woman in the above text was an impossible situation with man. She had an infirmity that in today's terminology would be identified as a terminal or a chronic disease. Her condition was pathetic. The scripture lets us understand that this woman had bled for twelve years without any medical solution, but she tried everything possible to no avail. We all have situations in our lives that we have attempted to resolve on our own in every way possible, but the problem stares and screams at us declaring it is impossible. However, to God be the glory! We serve the Almighty God who specializes in turning impossibilities into possibilities.

What was this woman's infirmity? Her infirmity was the issue of blood. What is your infirmity? The Greek word used for *"issue of blood"* is called **Haimorrheo** (Strong's G131). It is a compound word comprising **Haima** (Strong's G129), meaning *"blood,"* and **Rheo** (Strong's G4482) meaning *"to flow."* Haimorrhoeo, therefore means, *"to suffer from a flow of blood," "to have a discharge of blood,"* or *"to lose blood,"* from which the English word hemorrhage is obtained, which signifies *"to suffer from a flow of blood."* You or your loved ones may have had to suffer and experienced untold hardship, agony, and frustration. I want to declare upon you that as you believe and hold on to the report of the Lord, it shall be well with you in Jesus' name.

Now, let me share with you just some of the frustration and agony that this lady would have had to come to grips with as she suffered from the flow of blood for twelve years.

She Had an Issue of Blood for Twelve Years: The scripture declares in Leviticus 17:11 *"that the life of the flesh is in the blood."* This implies that as she lost blood, she was losing the life of the flesh that inevitably led to her losing strength in her body. Unbelievably true, gradually becoming emaciated and she must have lost her physical structure throughout the twelve years of her bleeding beyond the point of recognition. This must have been a traumatic experience for her. She must have become a societal misfit, economically bankrupt, and stigmatized in society because of her infirmity. Twelve years is no small number to suffer for the flow of blood. However, believing the report of the Lord will terminate every ailment in your life.

She Suffered Many Things From The Physicians: This implies that her ailment caused her to suffer many things and the discomfort she had to endure at the hands of physicians. She could have been used for various kinds of tests, while both quacks and genuine physicians practiced on her. They could have used her as a guinea pig to test their new medical drugs and therapies and as a study case for lobbying physicians. All of these and many unknown struggles that went through her subconscious mind must have profoundly devastated her and left her with no hope of recovering.

She Spent All That She Had: This implies that this woman became penniless because she sold everything she ever worked for or inherited in search of a medical solution to her predicaments. The infirmity ruined her financially. There are those who are struggling with their finances now because of the illness that has plagued their lives for too long as they search for solutions to their predicaments. Please, understand that God's report is for you to be whole in every aspect of your life. The Apostle Paul reiterates in Philippians 4:19, *"But my God shall supply all your need according to his riches in glory by Christ Jesus."* Indeed, God will!

Her Case Grew Worse: The physicians had tried all they could, but to no avail, they had given up on her. The woman did all she knew how to do or could afford but was nothing better as her case grew worse, the infirmity persisted with no hope of recovery. This became a nightmare that she was never to awaken from, and she was left at the mercy of her ailment, which was now gradually eating into the fiber of her being.

When she had heard of Jesus, came in the press behind, and touched his garment. (Mark 5:27). The scripture lets us understand that in her mess, she heard a message. What did she hear? Well, whatever she must have heard gave her hope in a hopeless situation, peace amid confusion and despair. I believe she heard that Jesus Christ is the Messiah, the Savior of the world. She understood that He walked upon the sea, healed the blind, raised the dead, cast demons out, cleansed the leper, and healed the disabled. "HE" is the Way, the Truth and the Life (Our Resurrection).

When she heard all about Jesus, there was a stirring in her inner being that caused her to conclude, "If only I can touch the hem of His garment, I shall be made whole." (See Mark 5:28). In other words, she <u>believed</u> what she heard (the report of the Lord). *"So then faith cometh by hearing, and hearing by the word of God."* (See Romans 10:17). She confessed God's Word for *"...with your mouth is confession made unto salvation"* (Romans 10:10) and she acted on the God's Word, *"... for faith without works is dead* (James 2:26)."

No matter the circumstances or the mountains confronting you, your impossibilities will become possible in the matchless name of Jesus Christ. Take time to hear, confess, and act on God's Word for the manifestation of what your heart's desire. For that which you hear and feed on will determine what you will confess and believe. That which you confess will determine your possession and that which you act upon determines your ultimate result. **God's Word works**. All that you need to do is to act upon it in faith.

What Could Have Stopped Her Miracle?

The Crowd roundabout Jesus Christ: Just the thought of going through this massive crowd surrounding Jesus could have stopped her from experiencing her miracle. Seeing this vast sea of people would have discouraged her instantly, but she made up her mind, and she was not going to be denied. The fact that she was able to get to where Jesus was showed her resolve to get the miracle that she desperately needed. Taking into consideration her condition, maneuvering her way through the multitude round about Jesus was another reality that she had to contend with.

So many things today seemingly want to stop us from our miracle. The crowd round about Jesus was one of those things that could have prevented this woman. What are those things that are standing as obstacles on your path and hindering you from your miracle today? Is it the crowd or unbelief? Despite what it is, you must be resolved not to allow anything or anyone to rob you of your miracle and breakthrough. Jesus Christ has already paid the price. All you need to do is to appropriate the finished work of Calvary upon your life.

Discouragement and Disappointment: She had tried everything at her disposal and did whatever she was required to do, but all to no avail. With her life gradually slipping away, without hope and no sight of her healing and deliverance, her situation was growing worse by the day.

The mental anguish she was subjected to, the lack of results despite all her efforts could have been so discouraging and disappointing that she should have stopped trying. Going on or being willing to try something new would have looked outrageous and ludicrous, but despite these challenges, she stepped out on faith.

In the same light, you should not allow discouragements and disappointments to stop you from believing God for whatever it is you are trusting Him to release into your life. It could be healing, the restoration of your finances or deliverance from the powers of darkness, no matter what believe and hold on to the report of the Lord in whatever situation and receive your miracles.

Having Bled for Such a Long Time, She Had No Strength to Push Her Way Through: This would have been a significant hindrance to her miracle. She could have concluded that there was no point in trying to elbow her way through the vicious crowd to where Jesus Christ was. After all, she was physically, mentally, and emotionally weak and depleted. Despite her weakness and seemingly impossible task of getting to where Jesus was, however, she was determined to act on what she had heard, and that is to touch the hem of Jesus' garment at least.

Do not give up on your miracle! Every step of faith you take draws you closer to the source of your miracle and breakthrough. Start today, just like that woman with the issue of blood. Be resolved on taking that step of faith toward your miracle, and you will not be disappointed. For if you act upon the report of the Lord, the arm of the Lord shall be revealed to you.

The Reports of Man and Physicians: This would have undoubtedly stopped her miracle if it were all she clung to. Holding on to the reports of men and the physicians, reviewing that diagnosis in her thoughts and allowing them to echo in her mind could have obliterated her determination to press on for her breakthrough and the miracle she so desperately wanted.

Man's report has a way of getting to us, but please do understand that man will always have a report about you and your circumstance, but consider man's report as man's report — no more, no less. In like manner, view God's report as God's report. Hold on to God's report, and you will receive your miracle.

The People's Opinion of Her Situation: Again, people will always have an opinion on your situation. What people thought about her and their evaluation of her condition could have stopped her from getting the miracle she so desperately needed. In your quest for whatsoever miracle, present all your cares, anxieties and problems to God in spite of man's opinion.

The Apostle Paul declares, *"Now unto him that is able to do exceeding abundantly above all that we ask or think, according to the power that worketh in us,"* (Ephesians 3:20). He can do *"exceeding abundantly above"* what you can imagine or think. Do not allow people's opinion of your situation to determine and define your reality. Allow God's Word to define your reality, set the parameter within which your life will gravitate and the standard by which you live your life daily. Just live by the report of the Lord.

You Are Loosed from Your Infirmity

"And, behold, there was a woman which had a spirit of infirmity eighteen years, and was bowed together, and could in no wise lift up herself. And when Jesus saw her, he called her to him, and said unto her, Woman, thou art loosed from thine infirmity". (Luke 13:11-12)

Whose report will you believe? Many people believe that God sometimes heals the sick. They know nothing about the many facts, which prove that physical health is part of our "Soteria" (salvation). They have no personal knowledge that *"Jesus Christ is still the same yesterday, today and forever."* (Hebrews 13:8). What Jesus did yesterday, He can also do today. He has not changed, and He will not change. It is crucial to be fully convinced that what Christ did back then, He can and will do today.

In the scriptural text above, it shows that Jesus heals a woman who had been crippled for eighteen years on the Sabbath day. Luke says she has a "spirit of infirmity" or a "sickness caused by a spirit" (Luke 13:11 NASB) or a "disabling spirit" (Luke 13:11 ESV) or is "crippled by a spirit" (Luke 13:11 NIV). Quite simply then, this "spirit of infirmity" is a **demon** who caused the woman to be disabled for eighteen years. We read that this spirit of infirmity had plagued this woman to the point where she was maimed and physically disfigured.

Your situation may or may not be as dramatic as the situation above. However, God can turn any case around and make the impossible possible. Whatever your infirmity, whether it is spiritual, physical, mental or otherwise, let it be known unto you that there are <u>no</u> infirmities, that will not respond in obedience to the authority of the name of Jesus Christ.

The Apostle Paul lets us understand in Philippians 2:10-11, *"That at the name of Jesus every knee should bow, of things in heaven, and things in earth, and things under the earth; And that every tongue should confess that Jesus Christ is Lord, to the glory of God the Father."* When you speak the Word of God in faith, every tongue will confess that Jesus Christ is Lord, and every knee will surely bow in submission to the authority and the power of His Word.

You must be prepared, by faith, to see beyond the circumstances and overcome all of these hindrances and much more that the enemy can and will bring against you on your quest for a miraculous breakthrough concerning your health, family, finances, business, ministry and everything that concerns you. The enemy cannot stop you unless you allow him to prevent you from experiencing your miracle. The enemy will try, but surely, he and his cohorts shall not prevail.

You have to hold on to the confession of your faith without wavering. (See Hebrews 10:23). Like the woman said, "If only I can touch the hem of his garment, I will be made whole." You see, she was more than determined to reach out for her miracle despite her situation. Your situation may not be as dramatic as this woman's situation. However, you must reach out in faith, believing the report of the Lord and that there shall be a manifestation of your miracle in Jesus name.

NOTHING IS IMPOSSIBLE

"And Jesus said unto them, Because of your unbelief: for verily I say unto you, If ye have faith as a grain of mustard seed, ye shall say unto this mountain, Remove hence to yonder place; and it shall remove; and nothing shall be impossible unto you." (Matthew 17:20)

In the scriptural text above, Jesus said, "If you have faith like that of a mustard seed and do not doubt, you can say to a mountain, 'Remove to yonder place' and it will move for **nothing shall be impossible for you.**" Nothing! That's it! Nothing shall be impossible if you dare to believe God's reports for your life. You may be going through some challenging moments right now. It could be your health, finances, or your relationship with your spouse. God's report declares <u>nothing</u> shall be impossible for you.

Take notice of the instruction that Jesus gave. He said unequivocally, **"Say."** He is instructing you to speak to, to declare upon the mountain, impossibilities, or challenges that militate against you. Do not be intimidated by what seems to be impossible in your life right now speak to that mountain in obedience to God's Word and is impossible will become possible to Glory of God.

There are times when what you <u>**say**</u> is more efficient and prevailing than when you are lamenting over the mountain of impossibilities. It is evident in the text above that instead of whining and complaining **about** the mountains of life; you should be audacious in **speaking to** them, commanding them to be removed. Take authority today and begin speaking faith-filled words to the mountains in your life and watch God turn your tears of sorrows into joy.

Jesus asserted that a spoken word of faith would give a believer absolute dominion and victory in every circumstance. Nothing is impossible for those who have learned not only how to pray, but even more, how to **say**. There is no difficulty insurmountable to those who can speak the command of faith.

BEHOLD, I WILL DO A NEW THING; NOW IT SHALL SPRING FORTH; SHALL YE NOT KNOW IT? I WILL EVEN MAKE A WAY IN THE WILDERNESS, AND RIVERS IN THE DESERT.

ISAIAH 43:19

Chapter Five

Whose Report Will You Believe?

God's Word Brings Change

So shall my word be that goeth forth out of my mouth: it shall not return unto me void, but it shall accomplish that which I please, and it shall prosper in the thing whereto I sent it. (Isaiah 55:11)

God's Word brings changes that are impossible for anyone or anything else to bring about. It is imperative to reiterate that God's Word has the innate capacity to bring about positive and lasting changes in your personal and professional life. For this simple reason, we must submit to the total counsel of God's Word as the final authority in our lives, individually and collectively as a people.

These changes could be drastic and instantaneous or spontaneous and simultaneous. However, in whatever manner these changes occur, we must rest assured that it will come to pass although it may tarry. You have to desire this change for it to come about. Just as the above text reiterates the word that goes out of the mouth of God will not return until it has brought the changes it was met to bring.

What areas of your life do you seek changes? Is it spiritual or physical? Let it be settled in your heart that the power of God's Word can and will bring changes to those areas of your life. All you need is one word from God, believing and holding on to the report of the Lord. As a result, the arm of the Lord will be revealed unto you.

> *"The entrance of thy words giveth light; it giveth understanding unto the simple." (Psalm 119:130)*

> *"The entrance and unfolding of your words give light; their unfolding gives understanding (discernment and comprehension) to the simple." (Amplified Bible)*

The reason there is so little light today in most believers is that they are no longer pursuing God's Word. At the entrance of God's Word, there is light. In other words, God's Word brings illumination and clarity to every aspect of our human existence. The light of God's Word will be experienced as we hear and yield to its prompting. We know that darkness is not just the absence of light, but darkness exists whenever and wherever evil is present and manifests its activities, and it is only God and his word that can furnish light in the darkness.

The scriptures declare in John 1:5, *"that light shineth in darkness; and the darkness comprehended it not."* Darkness is bound to dissipate in the presence of light. When the Word of God comes into your life, the light of God's glory reveals every hidden thing that contends with you, that is hindering your progress in life. God's Word is powerful and brings about changes in all aspects of your life by exposing the enemy's maneuvers and permanently destroying the works of darkness.

AT YOUR WORD

"Now when he had left speaking, he said unto Simon, 'Launch out into the deep, and let down your nets for draught'. And Simon answering said unto him, 'Master we have toiled all the night, and have taken nothing: nevertheless at thy word I will let down the net.'" (Luke 5:4-5)

The scripture lets us understand that the multitudes pressed about Jesus to hear the Word of God, and after He was through preaching and teaching God's Word, He spoke to Simon. After using Simon's boat as His podium to minister, He gave a command that was to change the fisherman's frustrations and disappointments, having toiled all night for fish to no avail. Simon's response to Jesus was parallel to what the Master had commanded. At the time of Jesus' command, the natural circumstances were unfavorable to the command, but his experience negates what could be if he obeyed the command that Jesus gave.

Another fact was that Simon and his colleagues had labored tirelessly through the night to no avail. They were frustrated, exhausted, and disappointed with the lack of results. It was also evident that it was at the wrong time of the day to be out fishing and, of course, these men were trained, skilled, and seasoned fishermen. It seemed ridiculous for Jesus Christ, the son of a carpenter who to them scarcely knew anything about fishing, to tell them to launch into the deep for a draught. However, Simon, in all of his confusions and frustrations, overlooked the opinion of the other fishermen present. He ignored his doubts and disappointments, even if it seemed improbable that they would catch anything, and he said, *"Nevertheless, at thy word, I will let down the net."*

"Nevertheless" signifies that nothing else is prompting him to do this. He has examined all the possibilities, and nothing seems to be to our advantage, and I have been through this before, but "nevertheless" at **YOUR WORD,** we will act with our confidence preconcerted on your command. There is power in the Word of God, and results occur when that Word is acted upon in faith. Whenever you are faced with setbacks, start claiming and declaring, "Nevertheless! Nevertheless!! Nevertheless!!!"

However high the mountains or how low the valleys, let God's Word be your firm foundation and your confidence. The scripture declares, *"For he spake, and it was done; he commanded, and it stood fast."* (Psalm 33:9) If our attitude is like that of Simon Peter, and we merely obey and act upon God's Word, irrespective of the cares and issues of life, we will experience supernatural changes that surpass human explanation.

Our father of faith, Abraham, had a situation of infertility. He deeply desired a change in this circumstance, but that change could not have been brought about by human efforts. In Genesis 15, God spoke to him and promised that He would make him a great nation, but at the time this Word was pronounced. The situation did not seem as if it would be possible. But in the fullness of time, according to God's report, it was fulfilled.

POWER OF THE SPOKEN WORD

> *"And when Jesus was entered into Capernaum, there came unto him a Centurion, beseeching him, And saying, 'Lord, my servant lieth at home sick of the palsy, grievously tormented.' And Jesus saith unto him, 'I will come and heal him.' The centurion answered and said, 'Lord, I am not worthy that thou shouldest come under my roof: but speak the word only, and my servant shall be healed. For I am a man under authority, having soldiers under me: and I say to this man, Go, and he goeth; and to another, Come, and he cometh; and to my servant, Do this, and he doeth it.'"* (Matthew 8:5-9)

The spoken Word of God will bring about tremendous changes in every area of our human existence. It possesses inherent power to accomplish and fulfill the purpose for which it was sent. The scripture lets us understand that *"A man's belly shall be satisfied with the fruit of his mouth; and with the increase of his lips shall he be filled. Death and life are in the power of the tongue: and they that love it shall eat the fruit thereof"*. (Proverbs 18:20–21). *It* is imperative for you to understand that you can do a great deal of good, or a great deal of hurt, both to others and to yourself, according to the use of your tongue. This is true because the words we speak exert great power, either positively or negatively. The scripture says that a man's belly is satisfied with the fruit of the mouth — death and life are in the power of the tongue.

As the disciples journeyed with Jesus across the sea one day, He was asleep in the lower chambers of the ship. There arose a storm against them, which caused the disciples to be so terrified that they declared to Jesus, "You do not care that we perish!" All Jesus did was to rebuke the storm by His spoken word, which brought immediate changes to that circumstance. Child of God, rest assured that Jesus Christ can and will rebuke the storms in your life today only believe.

THE WORD PREVAILS

"So mightily grew the Word of God and prevailed." (Acts 19:20)

God's Word has such potency that it prevails over every circumstance and situation. This power was so reliable that men were willing to give up their practices and destroy their curious arts to follow Jesus Christ as God's Word grew. God's Word increased, and the power of God was manifested as demonstrated by the extraordinary deeds that were wrought in and through the lives of the Apostles.

I cannot emphasize this enough: The degree to which God's Word grows in your life is the same degree that the Word will prevail in your life and to that same degree, you will exercise the power of the Word. The Word will prevail in and over your life, your will, your emotions, and your affections. It will overcome and prevail over all of the schemes and onslaughts of the enemy. Be assured that God's report will prevail over your personal and professional struggles.

POWER OF GOD'S PROMISE

"For as the rain cometh down, and the snow from heaven, and returneth not thither, but watereth the earth, and maketh it bring forth and bud, that it may give seed to the sower, and bread to the eater: So shall

my word be that goeth forth out of my mouth: it shall not return unto me void, but it shall accomplish that which I please, and it shall prosper in the thing whereto I sent it." (Isaiah 55:10-11)

As it declares in the book of Hebrews 6:13, *"For when God made promise to Abraham, because he could swear by no greater, he sware by himself."* As we examine Abraham's life, it is evident that the issues pending in his heart created an uncertain outlook, concept, and pursuit.

Nevertheless, all that changed at the evidence of a word of promise from God. I know many people can relate to Abraham and Sarah. They are experiencing issues on their journey of life, and this tends to shape our outlook on life. However, when we were able to locate a word of promise from God's Word, that becomes what determines our conduct and outlook in life. It is imperative to know that God made a promise and swore to bring that promise to fruition despite the circumstances of life. This is one of the fundamental truths that as children of God, we must grasp with certitude that God's Word is our ultimate guarantee.

Understand Child of God, that God's Word is His promise. Unlike man, God can fulfill what He has promised. The book of Numbers 23:19 let us know that. *"God is not a man, that he should lie; neither the son of man, that he should repent: hath he said, and shall he not do it? or hath he spoken, and shall he not make it good?"* The power to activate and accomplish His promise (His Word) is built within the promise. Hallelujah!

SO SHALL MY WORD BE THAT GOETH FORTH OUT OF MY MOUTH: IT SHALL NOT RETURN UNTO ME VOID, BUT IT SHALL ACCOMPLISH THAT WHICH I PLEASE, AND IT SHALL PROSPER IN THE THING WHERETO I SENT IT.

ISAIAH 55:11

Chapter Six

Whose Report Will You Believe?

Hope Comes Through God's Word

"As it is written, I have made thee a father of many nations,) before him whom he believed, even God, who quickeneth the dead, and calleth those things which be not as though they were. Who against hope believed in hope, that he might become the father of many nations; according to that which was spoken, So shall thy seed be. And being not weak in faith, he considered not his own body now dead, when he was about an hundred years old, neither yet the deadness of Sarah's womb: He staggered not at the promise of God through unbelief; but was strong in faith, giving glory to God;" (Romans 4:17-20)

Who against hope: Though an old man (Abraham) and his wife, an aged woman far beyond the time of childbearing, (Sarah) he yet believed the promise that he would have numerous offspring. The text above indicates that Abraham, against hope, believed in hope. What does this mean? It is evident, considering the passage above that there were what I would like to refer to as natural hope and supernatural hope in Abraham's situation.

The natural hope is that which comes as a result of facts. These are the arguments of sense, reasons, and experiences that are obvious in the natural. Their situation, however, was that of childlessness because Abraham and Sarah had long passed the age of childbearing. Against this inducement to the contrary, he believed in another kind hope, which was born as a result of the spoken Word, God's report. In our discourse, we will refer to natural hope as negative hope.

On the other hand, the supernatural hope is that which comes as a result of God's Word. This is what enabled him to see beyond natural inducement and rational grounds of impossibilities to God's all-sufficiency, the hope of becoming a father of many nations, according to God's Word. By faith, he would see the promise fulfilled in Sarah, his wife. This I will term as positive hope. Positive hope is that which defiles all else and anchors on the promises of God's Word.

Abraham and Sarah were well advanced in age, and Sarah had passed the age of childbearing (See Genesis 18:11). It was a hopeless situation that was indicated with all the available evidence. The situation gave them hope, which is the hope of impossibility. It cannot come about, and it is too late; time is of the essence now, and it is not your season. God spoke to Abraham, promising him a son. As a result of this promise from the Lord, hope was now born in Abraham's heart.

Therefore, the scripture lets us understand that against hope (negative hope, that natural hope, which are the arguments of the senses that sees it impossible), Abraham believed in hope (positive hope, that which sees it possible and that what God has said will come to pass irrespective of the present circumstance). Regardless of the deadness of Abraham and Sarah's bodies, God had a plan and a promise. You may have lost hope in your situation, but you have to understand that one word from God will change that situation for your good. When everything else fails, God's Word will <u>not</u> fail, and His Word is forever settled in heaven. Jeremiah, the Prophet, stated, *"Then said the Lord unto me, Thou hast well seen: for I will hasten my word to perform it."* (Jeremiah 1:12).

Consider this, Child of God: The scripture declares that *"Abraham was not weak in faith, he considered not his own body now dead, when he was about an hundred years old, neither yet the deadness of Sara's womb. He staggered not at the promise of God through unbelief; but was strong in faith, giving glory to God; And being fully persuaded that, what he had promised, he was able also to perform. And therefore it was imputed to him for righteousness."* (Romans 4:19-22) Weak faith is the result of giving consideration or meditation to the circumstances that faced you. To have strong faith, you must stay focused on God and His unchanging Word as the final arbiter for ALL of life's situations.

Unbelief is the foundation of our staggering at the promises of God. This causes us to be double-minded and unstable in our hearts. Strong faith is born as we stay focused on God's promises without wavering, with an ardent persuasion that God can do exceeding abundantly above all that we ask or think according to the power that works in us. God's Word brings hope to the hopeless despite the circumstance as the Word is received and acted upon.

When hope is lost, it means that the confident expectation and accomplishment of things not seen have been exchanged with impossibility, and this impossibility is now based on the experiences of the natural senses. It could be sickness, poverty, or an impossible situation in which you have lost hope. The first thing to do is to submit to God's Word and discover for yourself what He has said. Cast all your cares upon Jesus, hold on to the confession of your faith based on God's Word, and this, in effect, will restore hope to you regardless of the situation.

The dilemma of most Christians is that, often, they have confessed faith in the absence of hope. You see, brethren, it does not work that way. Faith is the substance of things hoped for. There have to be things hoped for. Faith will act to obtain what you are hoping for. Like faith, hope must be based on God and His word to achieve the results anticipated. When your hope is anchored in God's Word, there will be a performance, and a physical manifestation of the things hoped for.

Understand then that something that is seen is not hope. Hope is a firm assurance and expectation of things <u>not</u> seen. When something you are hoping for manifests in the natural, it is no longer hope. For instance, if I am hoping for healing and that healing manifests in the natural, I no longer hope for it because I have received it. Therefore, before the manifestation of what you are hoping for all you have to do is be thankful and keep confessing God's report concerning that situation, believing that you have received what it is that you are hoping. Be hopeful in all situations for the Lord will see you through if you faint not.

THE HOPE OF FULFILMENT VERSUS GOD'S DEMAND

> *"And it came to pass after these things, that God did tempt Abraham, and said unto him, 'Abraham': and he said, 'Behold, here I am.' And he said, 'Take now thy son, thine only son Isaac, whom thou lovest, and get thee into the land of Moriah; and offer him there for a burnt offering upon one of the mountains which I will tell thee of.' And Abraham rose up early in the morning, and saddled his ass, and took two of his young men with him, and Isaac his son, and clave the wood for the burnt offering, and rose up, and went unto the place of which God had told him".* (Genesis 22:1-3)

The hope of fulfillment cannot be circumvented because of God's demands, but rather, it consolidates and strengthens the realization of that which He said. After Isaac, the son of promise, was born, God asked Abraham to sacrifice him. This was an inconceivable and an unusual request for a man who had waited so long to have a child. It was through this child that the promise of becoming the father of many nations was to be accomplished.

It is interesting to note that Abraham's hope was not built on an illusion, but on the integrity of God's Word, knowing that God cannot back down on His Word. The covenant bond between them was so strong that Abraham obeyed God's request. As it were, it could have run through Abraham's mind that sacrificing his son will retard or destroy the hope of fulfilling God's promise upon his life and the promise for his entire generation. Having waited for such a long period before the child was born, he could have been skeptical about God's request.

However, the scripture declares in Hebrew 11:19 that he (Abraham) *"accounting that God was able to raise him, even from the dead; from whence also he received him in a figure."* This text lets us understand that Abraham was fully persuaded that God was able to raise his son, Isaac, even from the dead. The question of God not fulfilling His promise was beside the point. When your hope is genuinely predicated on God's Word, you will be willing to sacrifice all your Isaacs (precious things) to God to please Him without considering whether His promises will be accomplished in your life.

There is no doubt in your mind or heart that God will keep His promise, regardless of what the circumstances say. When God asks us to put our Isaacs on the altar, He gives us the privilege to experience Him as our sole provider **(Jehovah Jireh).**

THOU WILT SHEW ME THE PATH OF LIFE: IN THY PRESENCE IS FULNESS OF JOY; AT THY RIGHT HAND THERE ARE PLEASURES FOREVERMORE.

PSALM 16:11

CHAPTER SEVEN

WHOSE REPORT WILL YOU BELIEVE?

THE PLACE OF GOD'S WORD!

"Let the words of my mouth, and the meditation of my heart, be acceptable in thy sight, O LORD, my strength, and my redeemer." (Psalm 19:14)

"But what saith it? The word is nigh thee, even in thy mouth, and in thy heart: that is, the word of faith, which we preach." (Romans 10:8)

The Psalmist declared, *"let the words of my mouth and the meditation of my heart, be acceptable to you."* This implies a connection, a link, between the words of your mouth and the meditation of your heart. When the words of your mouth align with the meditations of your heart, there will be absolute results. We often don't receive or obtain the desired results because of the inconsistency and disconnection between the words of our mouths and the meditations of our hearts. (Saying one thing, but believing another.)

This is what the scripture means when it declares that *"out of the abundance of the heart the mouth speaks"*

(Matthew 12:34). It is not just what is in your heart, but the excess of what is in your heart, which, of course, is the result of what you have spent time meditating on. God's Word is to be found in our mouth and heart.

The mouth speaks what is in the heart. Romans 10:9 declare, *"That if thou shalt confess with thy mouth the Lord Jesus, and shalt believe in thine heart that God hath raised him from the dead, thou shalt be saved."* Often, this verse is used in Christian meetings and gatherings when the unsaved are praying the sinner's prayer as they give their lives to Christ.; this is appropriate usage of the scripture. However, we should not restrict it to the unsaved alone because that verse is loaded with benefits for the saved as well.

There are many benefits for the saved in that verse of scripture. If what you confess with your mouth corresponds with what you believe in your hearts, it will affect you either positively or negatively. The words which you speak can put you above or beneath, make or break you, give life or death, make you successful or a failure, give you victory or defeat. You can become a victor or a victim — the choice is yours.

LIVING IN THE AUTHORITY OF GOD'S WORD

"Forever, O Lord, thy word is settled in heaven."
(Psalm 119:89)

"For as the rain cometh down, and the snow from heaven, and returneth not thither, but watereth the earth, and maketh it bring forth and bud, that it may give seed to the sower, and bread to the eater: So shall my word be that goeth forth out of my mouth: it shall not return unto me void, but it shall

accomplish that which I please, and it shall prosper in the thing whereto I sent it." (Isaiah 55:10-11)

Many believers in the Body of Christ are not experiencing the authority and power of God's Word. The Psalmist declares that God's Word is forever settled in heaven. (See Psalms 119:89). It is not changeable or unstable. As God cannot change so, the Word, which he has spoken to his servants, will not change. No matter the circumstances, you must rest assured that His Word is settled concerning you. The importance of the believer living and experiencing the authority of God's Word in every area of life in this hour cannot be overemphasized.

As a believer, you must recognize that it is God's will for you to live in the authority of His Word and experience its promises. Child of God, God's Word <u>cannot</u> return to Him void until it has accomplished what it was sent for. As a result, you have to rest assured that God's Word possesses inherent power to bring to fruition His promises to you. Just as the scripture declares, *"And Jesus answered him, saying, It is written, That man shall not live by bread alone, but by every word of God."* (Luke 4:4)

The following dynamics must be built into your life to live in the authority of God's Word:

BY FAITH

There is an inherent power resident in the Word of God. To realize the potent, inherent, yoke-destroying and burden-removing power of faith, you must understand that it relates to God and the one who believes in Him. We may have experienced ups and downs, but that does not make void the power that faith produces. Your living in the authority of God's Word is predicated on *"as thou hast believed, so be it done unto thee."* (Matthew 8:13) Remember the story of the two blind men? Jesus said, *"according to your faith be it unto you."* (Matthew 9:29) Then, the scripture states, *"When Jesus heard it, he marveled, and said to them that followed, Verily I say unto you, I have not found so great faith, no, not in Israel."* (Matthew 8:10)

Faith is a vital component in experiencing and living in the authority of God's Word. Hebrews 11:6 says, *"But without faith, it is impossible to please him: for he that cometh to God must believe that he is and that he is a rewarder of them that diligently seek him."* Consequently, it is impossible to receive anything from God without faith, hence acquiring and developing your faith is necessary.

BY CONFESSION

> *That if thou shalt confess with thy mouth the Lord Jesus, and shalt believe in thine heart that God hath raised him from the dead, thou shalt be saved. For with the heart man believeth unto righteousness; and with the mouth confession is made unto salvation.*
> **Romans 10:9-10**

You can live in the authority of God's Word by confession. "By confession" denotes saying the same things that God's Word said about you and your circumstances. The Greek word for *confess* is **Homologéō** (Strong's G3670), and it is a compound word comprising **Homoû** (Strong's G3674), meaning *"same"* and **Lógos** (Strong's G3056), meaning *"something said," "to speak."* Homologeo, therefore, means, *"to speak the same thing as another,"* or *"to agree with"* or *"to acknowledge,"* to adopt the same style of speech, to speak alike. In our case, **"homologia"** means, *"saying the same thing God says," "speaking according to the report of the Lord which is His Word."* The importance of confession cannot be overemphasized in our walk with God. Therefore, it is crucial to learn to say exactly what God's Word is saying about you, even if your present reality is contrary to what the Word says.

If you confess with your mouth: This indicates speaking the same thing as another. Beware of this because you ultimately become what you confess. Hence, it is imperative that you must confess with your mouth what God's Word says about you, for when you do that, you agree with God and His Word. To obtain results, you need to believe in your heart what your mouth is confessing (progressively), as some may be saying one thing with their mouths and believing something else with their heart. The scripture lets us understand that *"...for out of the abundance of the heart the mouth speaketh."* (Matthew 12:34)

This implies that your mouth is the gateway of your heart. Hence, whatever proceeds out of your mouth should be in harmony with what is in your heart. This is where many Christians are missing it: confessing with the mouth without necessarily believing with the heart and vice versa. It is imperative to understand that there must be a connection between what proceeds out of the mouth and what the heart believes in bringing about manifestation. This combination works perfectly well together and achieves results.

BY THE SPOKEN WORD OF GOD

"Jesus saith unto him, Rise, take up thy bed, and walk. And immediately the man was made whole, and took up his bed, and walked: and on the same day was the Sabbath" (John 5:8-9).

Jesus here in the text above addressed the lame man at the pool of Bethesda and said to the lame man, "Pick up your bed and walk" and immediately was healed and made by the spoken word. The spoken Word of God will bring about tremendous changes in every area of our human existence, for it possesses inherent power to bring it to pass. The Scripture lets us understand that *"A man's belly shall be satisfied with the fruit of his mouth; and with the increase of his lips shall he be filled. Death and life are in the power of the tongue: and they that love it shall eat the fruit thereof"* (Proverbs 18:20–21).

There is power in and through the spoken Word of God. You can only experience the manifestation of the authority of God's Word when it is believed and spoken. Matthew 8:8 states, *"The centurion answered and said, 'Lord, I am not worthy that thou shouldest come under my roof: but speak the word only, and my servant shall be healed.'"* The centurion understood the power and authority of the spoken word. He realized he only needed Jesus to speak the word rather than embarking on a long journey. This also indicates that distance is no barrier in the realm of the spirit.

Matthew 8:16 declares, *"When the even was come, they brought unto him many that were possessed with devils: and he cast out the spirits with his word, and healed all that were sick."* Here, we see our Lord Jesus subdued as He cast out devils and healed the sick with His Word. You can only see the manifestation of the authority of God's Word when it is spoken and declared in faith. The centurion believed in the power of God's Word and experienced its manifestation. In like manner, you and I can experience and live in the authority of God's Word when it is spoken in faith.

WALKING IN THE SPIRIT

"This I say then, walk in the Spirit, and ye shall not fulfill the lust of the flesh." (Galatians 5:16) When we walk in the spirit, we are not connoting any spooky attitude, but merely walking by God's Word. Jesus declares the words that I speak to you are spirit and life. Consequently, when I walk in the spirit, I am walking in obedience to God's Word. It is in obedience to God's Word that I experience the demonstration of the authority and the power of His Word to set me free from every onslaught of the enemy.

BY PRAYER

Prayer is one of the keys that engenders living in the authority of God's Word. There is absolute power in prayer to disintegrate anything that could potentially hinder you from living and experiencing the authority of God's Word. Luke 18:1 states, *"And he spake a parable unto them to this end, that men ought always to pray, and not to faint."* Here, the text teaches that no matter the circumstance, we ought to persevere and be consistent in prayers and not give up or relinquish our prayer post.

In his epistle, James remarked, *"Confess your faults one to another, and pray one for another, that ye may be healed.*

The effectual fervent prayer of a righteous man availeth much. Elias was a man subject to like passions as we are, and he prayed earnestly that it might not rain: and it rained not on the earth by the space of three years and six months." (James 5:16-17). This caution indicates that there are times when we faint, possibly due to unanswered prayers, prevailing circumstances and so forth. However, in the face of these predicaments, if you want to live and experience the yoke-destroying and burden-removing power of God, you must persevere in prayers.

BY TAKING ACTION

James 1:22; 2:26 declares "But be ye doers of the word, and not hearers only, deceiving your own selves" and "For as the body without the spirit is dead, so faith without works is dead also" respectively. Living in the authority of God's Word demands that you act upon God's Word. It is of no importance what you <u>know</u> if you do not take action. Experiencing the authority of God's Word demands that you become a doer of the Word and not just a hearer or spectator. Act upon the Word of God and the Word of God will come through for you.

> **SO MIGHTILY GREW THE WORD OF GOD AND PREVAILED.**
>
> ACTS 19:20

Chapter Eight

Whose Report Will You Believe?

The Battle is Not Yours, but the Victory

"It came to pass after this also, that the children of Moab, and the children of Ammon, and with them other beside the Ammonites, came against Jehoshaphat to battle." (2 Chronicles 20:1)

"And the Philistine said to David, 'Come to me, and I will give thy flesh unto the fowls of the air, and to the beasts of the field.'" (1 Samuel 17: 44)

In the above texts, we shall be discussing two personalities of whom one is a king and the other a shepherd boy. *"And having spoiled principalities and powers, he made a shew of them openly, triumphing over them in it."* (Colossians 2:15). The church must realize that the devil has no weapons to fight, but he is still determined to fight the lost battle. The battles of life and against the church are becoming ferocious and very intense, like never before.

As a result, these battles have changed the course of many earnest Christians. Sometimes, most believers do not know what they ought to do. Instead, they easily yield to the rage of the enemy and get defeated before the battle even starts. This ought not to be so. Irrespective of the battle, you have to know that you are victorious and more than a conqueror. (See Romans 8:37). Just stand your ground! Again, I say, STAND YOUR GROUND!

Understanding that the battle is not yours will alleviate the stress and burdens of life that threaten to abort your purpose and destiny. King Jehoshaphat was afraid because of the imminent danger that loomed around his kingdom. He knew to go and wage war against his enemies without petitioning God and not assured of divine intervention would be a mistake. Therefore, he decided to set himself apart and do what seemed to be the foolish thing to do amid crises, as most people will assume. The king decided:

- To seek God
- To fast
- To pray
- To praise

In his petitioning, King Jehoshaphat reminded God of three essential things that you and I must always remember as we go before God in prayers:

1. The fatherhood of God
2. The sovereignty of God
3. The omnipotence of God

The king decided to trust the limitless God while recognizing his limitations. The king was limited in power and strength and did not know what to do, but he chose to depend on God for divine direction. When we are faced with imminent danger and the battle is raging, you have to understand that the battle is not yours, but the victory is yours. Do not allow man's report to destroy your confidence in God, but go to Him for direction and divine intervention. He will come through for you and all that concerns you. When you have sought the Lord in prayer, fasting, and praise, waiting for the answers to your prayers, you now have to position yourself in faith, believing that He that began a good work in you will bring it to pass. Stand still, brethren, and see the salvation of the Lord.

DON'T QUIT

"Let us hold fast the profession of our faith without wavering; (for he is faithful that promised);" (Hebrews 10:23).

"Let us hold fast the confession of our hope without wavering, for He who promised is faithful." (NKJV)

You may be on the verge of quitting on God, or you have already abandoned Him because of the events that have transpired in your life. Please, my brothers and sisters, do understand that quitters never win and winners never quit. I strongly admonish you not to abandon, for the scriptures make us know that we should hold fast the confession of our faith. We are to be consistent in speaking the same thing as God's Word, agreeing with and acknowledging Him in all things. The confession of your faith says you are healed, you are delivered, you are the head and not the tail, success and not a failure, and your going out and your coming in is blessed.

Let me remind you of the scriptural text that says, *"He (God) can do exceeding abundantly above all that we ask or think, according to the power that is at work within us."* (Ephesians 3:20) The word *"able"* is the Hebrew word **"yakol"**, which means *"to be able, to have power, having the capacity to prevail or succeed"* while the Greek word **"dunamai"** means *"to be able and to have power whether by virtue of one's ability and resources, to be able to do something, to be capable, strong and powerful."*

Child of God, understand God has the ability, the resources, the might and power to bring to fruition all that concerns you. Knowing and experiencing the ability of Jehovah will cause you to hold on, no matter the circumstances and despite man's report.

BLESS THE LORD, O MY SOUL, AND FORGET NOT ALL HIS BENEFITS: WHO FORGIVETH ALL THINE INIQUITIES; WHO HEALETH ALL THY DISEASES; WHO REDEEMETH THY LIFE FROM DESTRUCTION; WHO CROWNETH THEE WITH LOVINGKINDNESS AND TENDER MERCIES; WHO SATISFIETH THY MOUTH WITH GOOD THINGS; SO THAT THY YOUTH IS RENEWED LIKE THE EAGLE'S.

PSALM 103:2-5

Chapter Nine

Whose Report Will You Believe?

Not By Might, Not By Power But By My Spirit

"Then he answered and spake unto me, saying, This is the word of the LORD unto Zerubbabel, saying, Not by might, nor by power, but by my spirit, saith the LORD of hosts. Who art thou, O great mountain? Before Zerubbabel thou shalt become a plain: and he shall bring forth the headstone thereof with shoutings, crying, Grace, grace unto it" (Zechariah 4:6-7).

The above text stresses the divine power by which all opposition to the rebuilding of the temple will be removed. The great mountain here referenced are the mountains of opposition to the work both practical, personal and spiritual. Concerning you and your household, what are your mountains? What is that thing that seems huge, looming, hard to overcome, challenging to see past or seemingly impossible to climb? Is it a physical situation like maladies or other insurmountable challenges? Perhaps your mountain is unseen. Your mountain may be a hard marriage, childlessness, job loss, or unwanted divorce.

Have you ever gone through problems or adversities in your life and contemplate possible solutions that never resolved the situation and the troublesome thought of how you are going to get out of this situation. I am sure you have just as I have. It is imperative to note that we all go through exasperating situations in life, either personal or professional for which we long for individual encouragement and divine intervention from God. Very often, the thought of you ever getting out of trouble is inevitable as you encounter mountains that are so high, and the valley so low.

The text above helps us understand that no matter the oppositions that we face will not be resolved by might and power that is human strength of every description, physical, mental or moral, but by the Spirit of God which is the power of God. You have to come to the understanding that in despairing conditions, God is sufficiently able by his power to help you when there is no help from another, and this is the report of the Lord.

Man's report or the report of whatever mountain that confronts you, as the scripture declares that it is not by human might, nor by human power that you will overcome the challenges and oppositions that you face in life, but by the power of the Holy Spirit which is the Providence, and authority of God.

Be assured child of God that every mountain of difficulty that stands on your part to maximize potential and fulfilling your God-given destiny shall be made of non-effect. The power of God is available to you to dismantle any mountain of difficulty.

The following forces will help you deal with any mountain of difficulty.

The Force of God's Word: The Bible refers to "God's Word" as the driving force behind the creation of the universe. (See Genesis 1). The Bible declares in Jeremiah 23:29 that *"Is not my word like as a fire? saith the LORD; and like a hammer that breaketh the rock in pieces?"* Here we see the Holy Spirit likens God's Word to fire which is active, energetic, powerful and a mighty hammer that dismantles and disintegrates, what mighty forces are released when we are adequately engaged in faith! It is the Word of God that gives form and purpose to your life.

Therefore, declaring God's Word over that challenging situation confronting, you will dismantle that issue and ensures your victory. What this metaphor teaches is about the power of the Word of God that has the potential to change any situation that you are going through if when adequately engaged. The scriptures declare that God's Word goes forth out of his mouth will not return unto him void until it has accomplished that for which God blesses and prospers in that for which it has been sent. (See Isaiah 55:11). Consequently, as you engage the force of God's Word, you will be empowered to move insurmountable mountains in your life.

The Force of God's Promise: In Psalm 89:34, the psalmist stated unequivocally about the force of God's promise when he wrote *"My covenant will I not break, nor alter the thing that is gone out of my lips."* God's Word is spread with covenanted promises that cannot be destroyed because of the covenant. Hence, accessing and engaging this covenant promises will dismantle any mountain that will stand before you.

God swore by Himself and declared to Abraham, in blessing I will bless you, and multiplying I will multiply you. (See Hebrews 6:13-14). Therefore, if you stay with God, you will not lose your bearing in life. Whatever God has declared concerning you and your enterprise cannot and will not be subject to alteration. Locating and meditating on God's promise for your life will release the force of God's promises to destroy yokes and lift burdens and as a result, achieving outstanding results in your personal and professional life. The force of the promises of God will give you an advantage over the circumstances and issues of life.

The Force of Faith: The Word of God says *"For verily I say unto you, That whosoever shall say unto this mountain, Be thou removed, and be thou cast into the sea; and shall not doubt in his heart, but shall believe that those things which he saith shall come to pass; he shall have whatsoever he saith."* (Mark 11:23). The force of faith will eradicate any mountain, as you believe the report of the Lord.

The Holy Spirit further elucidated in Matthew 19:26 that: *"But Jesus beheld them, and said unto them, with men this is impossible, but with God all things are possible."* Our confidence should be predicated on God's Word knowing that with God all things are possible. You may have circumstances that are difficult from man's perspective; this should not trouble you because the scripture helps us understand that there are things that are beyond the realm of human possibility but not beyond God. Therefore, when you engage the force of faith, you will move mountains beyond your wildest imagination.

The Force of Prayer: Jesus teaches his disciples on the subject of prayer, said, *"And he spake a parable unto them to this end, that men ought always to pray, and not to faint.* (Luke 18:1). Where the warnings of Jesus helping us to understand that in other not faint we must keep the flame of prayers ablaze. Jesus in Matthew 26:41 instructs apostle Peter to pray for strength in overcoming temptation. The most potent energy anyone can generate is the energy and power generated through prayer. Furthermore, in Luke 6:12-13, Jesus demonstrates the importance of prayer in making significant decisions. Prayer helps us face and overcome all types of struggles.

In Psalm 107:28-30, the Psalmist writes: *"Then they cry unto the LORD in their trouble, and he bringeth them out of their distresses. He maketh the storm a calm so that the waves thereof are still. Then are they glad because they be quiet; so he bringeth them unto their desired haven."* Prayer is one of the fundamental forces that will help unlock your breakthroughs. Therefore, understanding the importance of prayers as the absolute power to disintegrate any insurmountable challenges is vital.

Here, the text above teaches that no matter how high the mountain and how low the valley that confronts you-you ought to persevere, stay focused and be consistent in prayers not giving up or relinquish your prayer post because the force of prayer will move that mountain on your behalf.

The Force of The Blood: The Bible declares *"And I heard a loud voice saying in heaven, Now is come salvation, and* strength, and the kingdom of our God, and the power of his Christ: for the accuser of our brethren is cast down, which accused them before our God day and night. and they overcame him by the blood of the Lamb, and by the word of their testimony, and they loved not their lives unto the death."* (Revelation 12:10-11). There is an inexhaustible power in the blood of Jesus Christ. Here the angels overcame by the power of the blood when they confronted the foes of darkness.

This same power is available to the church today. You can also overcome all the wiles and maneuver of the enemy as we confront the enemy and his cohorts by the power of the blood. As you learn to appropriate the power in the blood of Jesus Christ, you will see mountains, the host of darkness dismantled and its strategies rendered nonfunctional.

The Force of The Name of Jesus Christ: Apostle Paul in his letter to the Phillippi church stated: *"And being found in fashion as a man, he humbled himself, and became obedient unto death, even the death of the cross. Wherefore God also hath highly exalted him, and given him a name which is above every name: That at the name of Jesus every knee should bow, of things in heaven, and things in earth, and things under the earth; And that every tongue should confess that Jesus Christ is Lord, to the glory of God the Father."* (Philippians 2:8-11). There is an unquestionable power in the name of Jesus Christ. This name is above all names, whether in heaven, on the earth or underneath the earth and that every knee shall bow, in heaven, earth or underneath the earth and every tongue shall confess that He is Lord.

It is imperative that you come to the understanding that the name of Jesus is not magical in its application and dynamics, but in your relationship with Jesus, whose name you are invoking. The evil spirit answered the seven sons of Sceva saying, Jesus, I know, and Paul I know but who are you? (See Acts 1915). However, the name of Jesus is efficacious when adequately appropriated in faith based on the sacrifice of the finished work on Calvary.

Jesus obtained his name at **BIRTH** (See Matthew 1:21) and in Luke 2:21 the scripture declared *"And when eight days were accomplished for the circumcising of the child, his name was called JESUS, which was so named of the angel before he was conceived in the womb."* This text reveals that eight days after His birth and circumcision, the fulfillment of God's spoken Word through His Prophet Isaiah and Angel Gabriel concerning the name of the "Savior" of the world was fulfilled. Jesus Christ obtained his name by **CONQUEST** - That is as per the victory of over sin and death. (See Colossians 2:15). Jesus Christ obtained is named through **BESTOWAL** – That is, the Father conferred upon him a name above every other name as a result of the finished work on Calvary and as the Lord's sacrifice met the divine requirement for our wrenched souls that was damn to destruction. (Philippians 5:6-11).

The authority and power in the name of Jesus are evident in scripture as we see the early disciples testify to the power and authority of the name of Jesus. (See Luke 10:17). Jesus gave us the legal right to the use of His name; therefore, when we use the name of Jesus in contending for our faith, our victory is guaranteed. When you step into the arena of conflicts, it behooves you to employ the majestic name of Jesus Christ, for every knee must bow, and every tongue confess. This is the report of the Lord.

The Force of God's Faithfulness: The Bible tells us in Hebrews 10: 23: *"Let us hold fast the profession of our faith without wavering; (for he is faithful that promised;)."* God's faithfulness sustains everything, and we can entrust our lives upon God's faithfulness in times of imminent danger. God's Word lets us understand that God is a faithful God and we need to realize that God's faithfulness is not established on anything we have or can provide but on the absolute sovereignty of God himself.

It is incumbent upon us to know that God remains faithful even when we are unfaithful to him and to understand that his faithfulness produces a force that can dismantle any mountain in your life. The force behind God's faithfulness is predicated on his faithfulness to Himself, His word, His Son (Jesus Christ) and the Holy Spirit. In Psalm 89:33, the Psalmist writes, *"Nevertheless my loving kindness will I not utterly take from him, nor suffer my faithfulness to fail."* As a result, God cannot fail, and He will deliver what He has promised. Believing in the faithfulness of God will help you overthrow any mountain in your life.

The Force of The Anointing: *"And it shall come to pass in that day, that his burden shall be taken away from off thy shoulder, and his yoke from off thy neck, and the yoke shall be destroyed because of the anointing."* (Isaiah 10:27). The anointing is God's manifested presence, and it is the burden removing, yoke destroying the power of God. By the force of the anointing, every mountain that stands before you shall be destroyed. Therefore, to see the mountain remove and cast into the sea, you must engage the force of the anointing.

The scriptures declare that *"... for by strength shall no man prevail."* (See 1 Samuel 2:9), but by the power of the Spirit, and this is the report of the Lord. Therefore, believe and engage the report of the Lord today, and you will experience a demonstration of the arm of the Lord terminating troubling issues in your life. It shall be well with you and your household.

> GOD IS OUR REFUGE AND STRENGTH, A VERY PRESENT HELP IN TROUBLE. THEREFORE WILL NOT WE FEAR, THOUGH THE EARTH BE REMOVED, AND THOUGH THE MOUNTAINS BE CARRIED INTO THE MIDST OF THE SEA; THOUGH THE WATERS THEREOF ROAR AND BE TROUBLED, THOUGH THE MOUNTAINS SHAKE WITH THE SWELLING THEREOF. SELAH.

PSALM 46:1-3

CHAPTER TEN

WHOSE REPORT WILL YOU BELIEVE?

ENGAGING DIVINE CLEARANCE FOR SIGNS & WONDERS

> *"And David enquired at the Lord, saying, Shall I pursue after this troop? shall I overtake them? And he answered him, Pursue: for thou shalt surely overtake them, and without fail recover all". (1 Samuel 30:8).*

Divine clearance is a beautiful experience! Throughout this tremendous experience, you can gain access to divine instructions and guidance in the affairs of your life. In the above text, we discover that David seeks the Lord for divine direction and clearance after a devastating event in his life. This goes on to show that before you embark on the minor or significant endeavors in your life, it is of utmost necessity to seek the face of God for divine clearance and direction if you must experience signs and wonders in your pursuits. Therefore, engaging divine clearance for signs and wonders cannot be underestimated.

Men and women of old have experienced significant manifestations of the power of God in moments of insurmountable challenges and untold hardship. In these moments, we see God manifesting himself in diverse ways to protect, deliver, and set the captives free. These acts of God are referred to as signs and wonders of God Almighty and this they experienced as they obeyed and engaged God's divine clearance.

There are levels of signs and miracles that you will only experience as you heed divine instructions and clearance, which his God's report to you despite the prevailing circumstance. It is important to note that as you go through life, many things that may seek to draw you away from the things that are most important to you and as a result, you may have encountered untold hardship and errors of judgment in your life. Consequently, it is imperative that you become sensitive to divine clearance as this will empower you to step into the plans and purposes of God for your life.

DIVINE CLEARANCE DEFINED

Let us examine, the word DIVINE CLEARANCE: This word could mean many things to different people in this day and time, to varying stages of their lives, however for our subject matter we defined this word as the following...

- The divine permission that is given to you by God before you can embark on any assignment or action intended.
- The act of being impregnated with divine and specific information that releases you to do some of the things that you want to do.
- The God-given signal to GO, no inhibition or whatsoever, you are not limited by circumstances, favorable or not.

It is of utmost importance that whatever circumstance or situation we find ourselves, we need to obtain divine clearance, whether it is favorable in the sight of a man or not as long as you have permission from God to undertake that endeavor, signs, and wonders are guaranteed. Engaging divine clearance in your pursuit will empower you to walk in the promises of God as His divine clearance becomes the report of the Lord in your life.

It is vital that you understand that this divine clearance is not predicated on external events in your life, on individuals, your feelings, what you have or do not have, but on the absolute power of God and it has to come directly from heaven.

Agents of Divine Clearance

To hear from God and receive divine clearance, the following agents facilitate our access to the mind of God to gain access to God's mind and will for us. Let us now examine the following as the principal agents for divine clearance and guidance.

The Word of God – The Word of God serves an agent of divine clearance that is God speaking to you from the scripture and gives you instructions and directions as it pertains to everything concerning our lives. Getting divine clearance without God's Word is uncommon. Therefore, you must be an addict to the Word of God. Memorizing, meditating, studying, and reading the Word of God is of utmost importance if you gain divine clearance. Psalms 119:105, 2 Timothy 3:16

The Holy Spirit – The Holy Spirit is an agent of divine clearance. The spirit reveals to us the intents in the heart of god. The scripture states that the spirit of God guides us into all truth and shows us the things we do not know. Romans 8:14, John 16:13-15, 1 Corinthians 2:11

The Spoken Word – The spoken word is an agent of divine clearance. When the word is spoken, one can gain access to divine clearance. Jesus states that the word that I speak to yo; they are spirit and life. Therefore, you can receive spiritual insight into a situation and receive the solution to solve the problem, from the spoken Word of God. Romans 10:8

Testimonies - This can be an agent of divine clearance. This means listening to someone else's testimony or testimonies that can spark an answer for you and gain access to divine instructions that usher in new levels of experience and divine encounters.

Prayers - Through prayers, one can have a release to do what is one's heart or not do it. So, when you pray, God can give you access to the solution that you require to move ahead in your endeavors. David inquired in prayers on what to do, whether to pursue on not. He needed dive clearance that will ultimately guarantee his victory.

STEPS TO GAINING ACCESS TO DIVINE CLEARANCE

The following are the steps for gaining access to divine clearance

- Developing an intimate relationship with God
- Inquiring of God in prayers - 2 Chronicles 20:1-17

- Inquiring God for guidance - 2 Samuel 2:1
- Submit your will to the Lord - Luke 22:42
- In obedience to the Lord - Hosea 6:3

THE IMPORTANCE OF DIVINE CLEARANCE

And he said, O LORD God of my master Abraham, I pray thee, send me good speed this day, and shew kindness unto my master Abraham. Behold, I stand here by the well of water; and the daughters of the men of the city come out to draw water: And let it come to pass, that the damsel to whom I shall say, Let down thy pitcher, I pray thee, that I may drink; and she shall say, Drink, and I will give thy camels drink also: let the same be she that thou hast appointed for thy servant Isaac; and thereby shall I know that thou hast shewed kindness unto my master. And it came to pass, before he had done speaking, that, behold, Rebekah came out, who was born to Bethuel, son of Milcah, the wife of Nahor, Abraham's brother, with her pitcher upon her shoulder. Genesis 24:12-15

Here are just a few reasons why divine clearance is so necessary for your personal and professional life and the need for spiritual-awareness in divine approval. Understanding the importance of divine clearance is of utmost importance.

- One reason for divine clearance is it allows us to escape dangers, whether self-imposed, man-imposed, or spirit imposed. We would have several mistakes and significant errors of judgment that would have eternal consequences, but because of divine clearance, you will be delivered from the onslaught of the enemy.

- Another reason why divine clearance is essential is that it enables us to gain speed. Sometimes not knowing what action to take and what time to take that action could be very frustrating. But with divine clearance, it can mitigate against all that and take the guesswork and uncertainty out of the process. Certain things are not within our perception and realm of possibility that could sabotage our endeavor, and that can cause us temporary detours, but because of divine clearance, we have access to information, resources, and assistance that possibly we would not have gained if we had acted on our own accord.

- Divine clearance is necessary because it helps to facilitate and provide favorable conditions. In life, some struggles and frustrations are avoidable only by divine clearance. Favorable conditions that will be a figment of your imagination become your experience just because you are following and obedient to divine permission from God.

- The importance of divine clearance cannot be overemphasized because it enhances your profitability in any enterprise. Men have lost great relationships, businesses, family, and many setbacks merely because they went out in pursuit of profits without divine direction. However, your profitability is significantly enhanced as you are engaging divine clearance following instructions from God.

- One other reason why divine clearance is essential is that it helps to secure divine backing. God is not obligated to back what he has not given you clearance for and for you to ensure heavenly support, protection, or provision, it is imperative to respond to God's instructions.

- The last but not the least is divine clearance releases amazing breakthroughs and exploits. Isaiah 48:21 declare *"And they thirsted not when he led them through the deserts: he caused the waters to flow out of the rock for them: he clave the rock also, and the waters gushed out."* On their way to the promised land and because it was by divine clearance, they experienced breakthroughs that were only a figment of their imaginations.

Whose report you believe will determine whose power will prevail in your life. Today I prayerfully admonish you to believe the report of the Lord, and there will never be any better yesterdays in your life.

KINGDOM COVENANT PARTNER

Living Stone World Worship Centre, "One God One Family, One Destiny" a.k.a. New Creation Life Ministries is a ministry that is on the cutting edge of what God is doing in these last days.

> *"But thou shalt remember the LORD thy God: for it is he that giveth thee power to get wealth, that he may establish his covenant which he sware unto thy fathers, as it is this day" (Deuteronomy 8:18).*

The Scripture makes us understand that the only purpose in the heart of God when He gave us the power to obtain wealth was and is to enable us to become partners in establishing the covenant, which He swore to our fathers.

With this piece of truth, I sincerely urge you to rise to the purpose for which you have been empowered by becoming a covenant partner spiritually and financially today.

Your prayer and financial support will bless and enable someone to hear the gospel of our Lord Jesus Christ.

To request your free no-obligation KINGDOM COVENANT PARTNERS' information, please contact:

> Living Stone World Worship Centre
> "One God, One Family, One Destiny"
> A.k.a. New Creation Life Ministries

P.O. Box 30
1200 Brussels
Belgium

E-mail: apostle@livingstoneworld.org

Websites: www.livingstoneworld.org

ABOUT THE AUTHOR

Dr. Richard Onebamoi is an apostle by divine calling, an author, a business consultant, a leadership alignment strategist, and a success facilitator. Dr. Onebamoi is the founder and senior pastor of Living Stone World Worship Centre, "One God, One family, One Destiny," located in Brussels, Belgium. Dr. Onebamoi is also a certified coach, speaker, and trainer for The John Maxwell Team. Furthermore, he is the Founder of Men of Visionary Excellence (M.O.V.E).

Dr. Onebamoi is the founder and executive facilitator of The ROCK Consulting Group, with a mandate to inspire your performance, expand your imagination, cultivate your dreams, empower your success, and help you discover, develop, and maximize your God-given potential. He can provide leadership, success motivation, and educational and positive personal development training that will maximize potentials and minimize liabilities.

A vibrant and charismatic minister and highly sought-after conference speaker and published author of several books, including *Success Power Points*, *Kingdom Principles on Leadership*, *Whose Report Will You Believe?*, *Anatomy Of Frustration,* and *Winning Ways for Success*. Dr. Onebamoi carries an apostolic grace upon his life, an anointing to bring change to the lives of his listeners. He has a profound and unique insight into God's word. As he ministers around the globe, God continually marks his ministry with the demonstration of the Holy Spirit, transforming lives by the Word of His power.

Dr. Onebamoi is happily married to Catherine K. Onebamoi, who co-pastors with him and the associate executive facilitator of The ROCK Consulting Group and Richard Onebamoi International (ROI). They are blessed with four children, and they reside in Brussels, Belgium in the heart of the European Union.

Richard Onebamoi welcomes the opportunity to minister in churches, seminars, conventions, retreats, or men's, women's and youth groups. Contact at Richard:

Richard Onebamoi
P.O. Box 30
1200 Brussels
Belgium

Email: info@richardonebamoi.com

Website: www.richardonebamoi.com

www.richardonebamoibooks.com

Learn more about Richard at

amazon.com/author/business

Thank You

A Big thank you to you for purchasing and downloading my book and reading it to the end. If you enjoyed this, book or learned from it and found it useful. I would be very grateful if you would post a short review on Amazon. Your support does make a difference, and I read all the reviews personally so I can get your feedback and make this book even better.

Please take a moment of your time to leave a review for this book on Amazon.

www.ingramcontent.com/pod-product-compliance
Lightning Source LLC
Chambersburg PA
CBHW051347040426
42453CB00007B/454